Schwerpunktthema

Abitur Englisch

The Truman Show

Cornelsen

The Truman Show

von Christiane Mayer und Henning Sonntag

Verlagsredaktion

Ingrid von der Felsen-Ferguson

Layout und technische Umsetzung

Pamela May, May + Steinmüller, Designbureau, Berlin

Umschlaggestaltung

havemannundmosch, bureau für gestaltung, Berlin

www.cornelsen.de

Die Links zu externen Webseiten Dritter, die in diesem Lehrwerk angegeben sind, wurden vor Drucklegung sorgfältig auf ihre Aktualität geprüft. Der Verlag übernimmt keine gewähr für die Aktualität und den Inhalt dieser Seiten oder solcher, die mit ihnen verlinkt sind.

1. Auflage, 1. Druck 2009

Alle Drucke dieser Auflage sind inhaltlich unverändert und können im Unterricht nebeneinander verwendet werden.

Druck: CS-Druck CornelsenStürtz, Berlin

ISBN 978-3-06-032282-4

Inhalt gedruckt auf säurefreiem Papier aus nachhaltiger Forstwirtschaft.

Contents

» *Präsentiert von dem Sender, der niemals schläft, sehen Sie live und ungeschnitten – 24 Stunden am Tag und sieben Tage in der Woche – auf der ganzen Welt – mit Truman Burbank als Truman Burbank – aufgenommen im größten Studio der Welt – in einem von nur zwei menschlichen Bauwerken, die man aus dem Weltraum sehen kann: das andere ist die chinesische Mauer – die längste Dokumentar-Soap in der Geschichte – nun bereits im 30. Jahr –* The Truman Show*! ...* «

Liebe Schülerinnen und Schüler,

in diesem Heft finden Sie Vorschläge zur Auseinandersetzung mit *The Truman Show*.

Die Ansage *'Truman Burbank als Truman Burbank'* verrät bereits die Tragik des Hauptdarstellers: Truman Burbank ist Star einer beliebten Fernsehserie und wird rund um die Uhr von 5.000 Kameras beobachtet ... ohne dies zu wissen! Truman (*a true man!*) ist der einzig echte, wahre und aufrichtige Charakter in der Show, alle anderen sind wie Meryl (*merely!*) bloße Schauspieler. Sie spielen Gefühle wie Freundschaft und Liebe, sie täuschen sie nur vor und handeln nach den Vorgaben von Christof, dem Erfinder dieser Dokumentarserie. Das wird besonders deutlich, als Truman auf seinem Hochzeitsfoto die gekreuzten Finger seiner Frau Meryl sieht oder als er den Rat seines Freundes Marlon einholen will und dieser nur die Regieanweisungen umsetzt, die ihm über Kopfhörer gegeben werden. Erst als sich die Pannen der Regie häufen, realisiert Burbank, dass etwas in seiner Welt nicht stimmt, wird zunehmend misstrauisch und beginnt Fluchtpläne zu schmieden.
Damit kritisiert der Film ein zwar fiktives, aber angesichts der *reality shows* im Fernsehen durchaus denkbares Szenario. Es stellt sich die Frage, inwieweit ein Individuum – je nach der Vorstellung der Regisseure und Produzenten von Reality-TV-Serien – zu einer drehbuchgerechten Figur geformt werden kann und darf und letztendlich auch, was Realität eigentlich ist.
Darüber hinaus problematisiert der Film aber auch die zunehmende Vermarktung von Produkten durch sogenanntes *product placement* im Fernsehen oder die zunehmende Überwachung der Bevölkerung durch die immer weitergehende Erhebung und Archivierung von Daten über uns alle bis hin zum „gläsernen Bürger". Diese über den Film transortierte Problematik sollte im Rahmen der Diskussion des Films thematisiert werden.

Dazu werden im ersten Teil des Heftes zunächst weitere grundlegende Informationen zum Film gegeben.
Anschließend geht es in *Let's watch the film* zunächst um die Erarbeitung der Handlung. Neben einem *Scene index*, in dem die einzelnen Sequenzen mit Zeitangaben inhaltlich knapp zusammengefasst sind und der auch zur späteren Auffindung von Schlüsselszenen dienen soll, gibt es inhaltliche Fragen zum Film, anhand derer das grundsätzliche Verständnis abgeklärt werden kann.

Schließlich können Sie anhand der Bearbeitung des Worksheets *How Truman smelled a rat* nachvollziehen, aufgrund welcher zentralen Ereignisse sich Trumans Misstrauen langsam entwickelt und warum er letztlich den Entschluss fasst, trotz seiner Aquaphobie mit dem Boot aus Seahaven zu fliehen.
Im dritten Teil des Arbeitsheftes (*Let's analyse the film*) steht die eigentliche Filmanalyse im Vordergrund. Hierzu haben wir Worksheets entworfen, anhand derer erarbeitet wird, wie die Hauptfiguren mithilfe filmischer Mittel charakterisiert werden. Es sollen konkrete *stills* und einzelne Filmszenen analysiert werden, sodass deutlich wird, wie mit Einstellungsgrößen (*camera range*), Kameraperspektiven (*camera perspectives*), der Kamerabewegung (*camera movement*), dem Filmschnitt (*cuts*), dem Ton und dem Licht (*lighting*) ganz gezielt Effekte erreicht werden. Dazu können Sie auf das ▸ Worksheet *Selected terms for film analysis* www.cornelsen.de/abi-e (dort das *Truman*-Cover anklicken) zurückgreifen. Zugleich geht es immer auch darum, die Filmaussage nicht zu vergessen und das Verhalten der Figuren und deren Handlungsmotivation kritisch zu hinterfragen und zu bewerten.
Auch wenn es möglich ist, gezielt Schwerpunkte zu setzen und nicht alle Worksheets zu bearbeiten, lohnt es sich auf jeden Fall, die „Wiedervereinigungsszene" zwischen Truman und seinem Vater intensiv zu untersuchen, da gerade in dieser Szene (durch Christof) deutlich wird, wie filmische Mittel ganz bewusst eingesetzt werden, um die Zuschauer zu manipulieren.
Neben den Hauptfiguren waren uns außerdem die Thematisierung der Aspekte *product placement* und *utopia* besonders wichtig, da auch sie für den Film zentral sind.
Im letzten Teil des Arbeitsheftes (*Evaluation*) steht die abschließende Auswertung im Vordergrund. Sie geschieht zunächst inhaltlich, indem Sie unter Rückgriff auf die im dritten Teil erarbeiteten Ergebnisse eine abschließende Rollendiskussion vorbereiten: Sie werden mit Fragen der anderen Figuren konfontiert und müssen Rede und Antwort stehen. Im Anschluss sollte dann anhand einer *film review* und eines Interviews mit dem Regisseur Peter Weir der gesamte Film noch einmal gewürdigt werden.

Schließlich noch ein Hinweis: Bei der Beschäftigung mit dem Film empfehlen wir die Arbeit mit einem ▸ *viewing log*. Wahrscheinlich haben Sie Erfahrung mit der Nutzung eines *reading log* beim Umgang mit komplexen Texten. Bei der Filmanalyse ist es besonders notwendig, beim Anschauen des Films Informationen zu speichern, da es hier viel umständlicher ist „zurückzublättern" als in einem Buch. Praktische Hinweise zu *Working with a viewing log* finden Sie auch unter www.cornelsen.de/abi-e.
Unter dieser Adresse finden Sie auch ▸ Lösungen/Lösungsvorschläge zu einzelnen Aufgaben im Heft, die Sie bei Bedarf abrufen und für sich prüfen können.

Gutes Gelingen wünschen

Christiane Mayer | Henning Sonntag

The Truman Show (1998)

Directed by	Peter Weir
Writing credits	Andrew Niccol
Produced by	Scott Rudin Andrew Niccol Edward S. Feldmann Adam Schroeder

Cast

Jim Carrey	Truman Burbank
Laura Linney	Meryl Burbank (Hannah Gill)
Noah Emmerich	Marlon (Louis Coltrane)
Natascha McElhone	Lauren (Sylvia Garland)
Ed Harris	Christof
Holland Taylor	Truman's Mother
Brian Delate	Truman's Father
Peter Krause	Lawrence
Paul Giamatti	Control Room Director
Harry Shearer	Mike Michaelson
Philip Baker Hall	Network Executive

Chapters

1 A day in a life
2 Day 10,909
3 Aquaphobia
4 The chef's pal
5 Dreaming of Fiji
6 Memories of dad
7 Lauren ... or is it Sylvia
8 Paranoia
9 There's no place like home
10 Travellers beware
11 Lady ... flowers ... dented Beetle
12 I'm being spontaneous!
13 Blocked at every turn
14 Mococoa ... it's the best!
15 Father and son reunion
16 Trutalk
17 Do you think he knows?
18 He's gone.
19 Setting sail
20 Cue the storm
21 The sky's the limit
22 Who am I?
23 Good afternoon, good evening and good night
24 Credits

The plot

Truman Burbank, the main character of the film *The Truman Show*, is employed at an insurance company and married to Meryl, a nurse. Both live in Seahaven, an island paradise that has been voted the 'best place to live'. They lead a seemingly ordinary and unspectacular middle-class life, but what Truman does not know is that he is the star of a hugely popular 24-hour-a-day TV series, which has grown over the years into a billion-dollar franchise for the TV network and that in this real-time documentary every moment of his life is captured by about 5000 concealed cameras and broadcast to a giant global audience. All his friends and family are merely actors directed by Christof, the creator of the show. So Truman's whole life is fake.
As both the illusion and the ratings will collapse if Truman ever leaves Seahaven, the makers of the show have always staged elaborate events to make sure that Truman stays. Thus they are responsible for Truman's aquaphobia through having made his father 'drown' in a storm when Truman was a little boy, a means to keep Truman on the island. Moreover, Truman is constantly reminded of how wonderful Seahaven is compared to the dangers, dirt and problems that exist in other parts of the world. Whenever someone, like Lauren, intrudes to inform Truman of his zoo-like environment they invent an excuse to write people out of the script.
However, at the age of 30, his growing suspicions that develop because of certain flaws betrayed by the cast and the makers of the show make Truman curious enough to try to leave. In order to make him stay, Christof has to constantly devise new and increasingly absurd ways to thwart Truman's escape attempts.

Questions on the film

- What kind of person is Truman? Write a brief description of his character.
- When Truman is about to leave the show, Christof tells him that there is no more truth out there than there is in the world he created for him. The same lies, the same deceit. But in his [Christof's] world he has nothing to fear.
  Comment on this statement.
- Do you find the film convincing? Can you imagine that it is possible to keep a person in a fake world like Seahaven for 30 years and deceive him/her?
- The film criticizes the development of *Reality TV*. Compare *The Truman Show* with other Reality TV programmes you know and state similarities and differences.
- Imagine you were offered a role in *The Truman Show*. Consider the pros and cons of becoming a member of the cast.
- The film can also be said to deal with the problem of media addiction. What scenes might refer to this and how is this media addiction made apparent by film techniques.
- How does the film make it clear that *The Truman Show* has been very popular for nearly 30 years?
- Truman is 'on air' for 24 hours a day, 365 days a year, and they even plan the world's first 'on air' conception, although Article 12 of the UN Charter of Human Rights says that no one shall be subjected to arbitrary interference with his privacy, family, home or correspondence, nor to attacks upon his honour and reputation. Everyone has the right to the protection of the law against such interference or attacks. On the other hand the 1st Amendment to the American Constitution regulates that Congress shall make no law [...] abridging the freedom of speech, or of the press [...].
  Would you say that Truman could and should sue the makers of this show for denying him the privacy guaranteed by the UN Charter despite the 1st Amendment to the American constitution? Give reasons for your opinion.
- The 'Yellow Press' regularly informs people about the lives, affairs and problems of celebrities. Do you think people have the right to learn everything about the private lives of celebrities, or does this – in your opinion – contradict the right to privacy?
- How does the film illustrate Truman's growing doubts that something is wrong with his world?
- *The Truman Show* is not only a reality TV show, but also a 24-hour advertisement. How and what does it advertise?
- The film is often called a satire. Which sequences/episodes would you consider satirical? Why?
- Truman is watched 24 hours a day without knowing it. But we are also being watched and monitored, and others know more about us than we might think. Consider when and where such monitoring takes place and discuss whether it affects the right to privacy and data protection or whether it is a necessity.
- How does the film show that spectators are manipulated by the media? Would you say that we – as spectators or readers – are manipulated by the media too? What can we do to avoid such manipulation?
- How does the film illustrate the different relationships between Truman, his parents, Meryl, Marlon, Lauren and Christof, the creator of the show?

Scene index

Chapter (Time)	Characters / Action
1 Opening credits / Introduction: A day in a life	
0:00:00–2:02:37	Christof, director of The Truman Show comments on the show's realism: *There is nothing fake about Truman himself ... It isn't always Shakespeare, but it is genuine. It's a life.*
0:00:48–0:02:37	Truman talks to himself in the bathroom; Meryl and Marlon are introduced and also comment on the realism of the show: *It's a noble life, it's a blessed life.* (Meryl) *Nothing is fake, it's merely controlled.* (Marlon)
2 Day 10,909	
0:02:38–0:03:48	Truman on his way to work is greeted by neighbours. A large glass object falls from the sky and lands with a crash only a few inches from Truman's car.
0:03:49–0:05:28	Truman drives to work. A radio reporter mentions that a plane has lost parts over Seahaven. Truman stops to buy a newspaper and a magazine, allegedly for his wife and talks to adult twins.
0:05:29–0:06:32	Truman's office: he is secretly doing enquiries on a person called Sylvia or Lauren Garland, but she doesn't seem to be listed. Truman tears out the eyes of a woman's photo in the magazine he has just bought.
3 Aquaphobia	
0:06:33–0:08:46	Truman is sent to Harper Island by his boss. When he is at the ferry terminal and walks along the jetty he becomes paralysed. He stops completely when he sees a sunken boat and returns.
4 The chef's pal	
0:08:47–0:09:20	Truman is working in the garden when his wife arrives home. She shows a kitchen utensil she received for free.
5 Dreaming over Fiji	
0:09:21–0:11:02	Marlon presents a can of beer. While he and Truman are hitting golf balls along an unfinished bridge, Truman talks about his travel plans to Fiji.
6 Memories of dad	
0:11:03–0:12:46	Truman sitting on the beach. Flashback of the episode when he was out with his dad in a boat. A storm came up, Truman's father fell from the boat and drowned despite Truman's desperate efforts to rescue him. Back on the beach a shower directly rains on Truman, he jumps from side to side and is followed by the shower.
0:12:47–0:13:40	Truman informs Meryl about his plans to leave Seahaven. She tells him to be reasonable and finally tries to be seductive.
0:13:41–0:13:54	Viewers: Two car-park attendants are watching the show and commenting on it. They complain that they *never see anything.*
0:13:55–0:15:25	The next morning: Truman buys a newspaper and a magazine 'for his wife' again. On his way to his office he meets his dad, but when Truman wants to talk to him, he is dragged into a bus and taken away. Truman tries to follow him – in vain.
0:15:26–0:16:33	Truman is talking to his mother about the incident. She insists that his dad is dead.

Chapter (Time)	Characters / Action
7 Lauren ... or is it Sylvia?	
0:16:34–0:17:14	Truman opens an old trunk containing items from his childhood.
0:17:15–0:18:05	Meryl appears. Truman pretends to be fixing the mower and Meryl seems to advertise again.
0:18:06–0:18:26	Truman is alone again. He reopens the trunk and becomes thoughtful when seeing his old things.
0:18:27–0:18:46	Two waitresses in the Truman Bar. The ladies comment on Truman's behaviour.
0:18:47–0:21:06	10,190 days running – flashback Truman and Marlon in a college band. Truman gets to know Lauren, whose real name is Sylvia, but Meryl interferes. Later at a college dance Lauren appears again, but before Truman can get into contact with her two men hustle her away.
0:21:07–0:24:25	Flashback continues. Truman is preparing for his finals in the library. He meets Lauren again and they make an immediate appointment because Lauren acts strangely.
0:24:26–0:25:22	Flashback continues. They go to the beach and kiss each other.
0:25:23–0:26:45	Flashback continues. A car appears and a man who claims to be Lauren's father drags her into the car. Lauren tries to warn Truman that nothing is as it seems and tells him that her real name is Sylvia. Truman is alone on the beach holding her red scarf.
0:26:46–0:27:05	Two waitresses in the Truman Bar comment on Truman's behaviour.
0:27:06–0:28:12	Truman tries to reconstruct a picture of Lauren. He uses Meryl's picture as a hide.
0:28:13–0:28:17	Brief shot of Lauren watching Truman.
8 Paranoia	
0:28:18–0:29:27	Truman is on his way to work and hears mysterious voices from the radio. The voice seems to describe his route – suddenly people are acting strangely.
0:29:28–0:32:07	Truman walks to his office, but changes his mind and begins to walk around the town. He behaves as if he was being watched, runs in front of a bus and stops a car.
0:32:08–0:33:10	Truman enters a building and discovers a secret room of the set behind a lift. He is thrown out of the building.
0:33:11–0:34:40	Truman appears in the shop where Marlon works and makes Marlon follow and talk to him.
0:34:41–0:35:26	Truman and Marlon on the beach – Truman tells his friend that he is going to go away for a while.
9 There's no place like home	
0:35:27–0:36:48	Meryl, Truman and his mum are looking at photos of Truman as a child and also of his wedding with Meryl.
0:36:49–0:37:37	Truman continues looking at the photos when Meryl takes his mum home. He discovers that Meryl kept her fingers crossed on one of the wedding photos.
0:37:38–0:40:50	Sunrise: Meryl is on her way to work. Truman wants to talk to her, but she pretends to be in a hurry. Truman follows her in his pyjamas to the hospital, where the staff try to stop him. The viewers see that the operation Meryl is in is not real.
10 Travellers beware	
0:40:51–0:42:03	Truman wants to book a flight to Fiji in the travel agency, but there are no flights for a month.

Chapter (Time)	Characters / Action
0:42:04–0:43:35	Truman is at the bus station from where he wants to get to Chicago. However, the bus does not leave because of engine trouble.
0:43:36–0:43:48	The Truman Bar: Visitors are discussing why Truman wants to go to Chicago.
11 Lady … flowers … dented Beetle	
0:43:49–0:45:47	Meryl comes home from work and approaches Truman in his car. Truman predicts that in a minute they will see a lady on a bike followed by a man with flowers and a dented VW-Beetle. He can make this prediction, because they come round and round in a loop.
12 I am being spontaneous	
0:45:48–0:47:56	Truman decides to be spontaneous and leave Seahaven. He seems to be weird when driving. Suddenly there is a traffic jam. Truman pretends to calm down, drives back, changes his mind again and finds that there is no traffic jam any more.
0:47:56–0:49:06	Truman overcomes his aquaphobia and crosses the bridge.
13 Blocked at every turn	
0:49:50–0:50:47	After crossing the bridge Truman and Meryl meet various obstacles like a fire wall and a police blockade because of an alleged accident at Seahaven's power station. When a police officer calls Truman's name, he panics, runs away terrified and is finally caught.
14 Mococoa … it's the best!	
0:50:48–0:53:08	Home again: Truman notices Meryl doing another ad. Truman and Meryl quarrel and Meryl calls a hidden cam for help, which makes Truman even more suspicious. Marlon arrives and gives comfort to Meryl.
15 Father and son reunion	
0:53:09–0:58:37	Truman and Marlon are at the end of the unfinished bridge talking about the things that happened: Marlon – prompted by Christof – tells Truman about their past and his 'true' feelings. Moreover, he tells Truman that he has found his father for him. Truman walks toward his father while Christof and his crew are preparing this reunion for the viewers. Everything ends in embraces, tears and emotions. Christof is being congratulated.
16 Trutalk	
0:58:38–0:58:53	Sylvia is in her flat watching Truman
0:58:54–1:00:08	Brief sequences of Truman's life and of the development from his birth to the present state are interrupted by: Truman drinking cocoa and shots of the biggest studio in the world. Then Michaelson announces *Trutalk* and an interview with Christof.
1:00:09–1:06:08	In the interview Christof reveals the concept of the story. He mentions that Meryl will leave Truman and that a new romantic episode, most probably with the first online conception, is waiting. The interview is interrupted with scenes of Truman's past showing how they successfully managed to keep him in Seahaven. Sylvia phones and argues with Christof about Truman. She accuses him of keeping Truman as a prisoner.
1:06:09–1:07:07	A viewer is seen. A TV is showing the sleeping Truman, Christof is standing next to him gently touching Truman's face on the huge screen.

Chapter (Time)	Characters / Action
17 Do you think he knows?	
1:07:08–1:08:35	Truman in his bathroom talking to himself in the mirror. The crew presume that he is back to his old self.
1:08:36–1:09:23	Truman leaves the house. He greets his neighbours and goes to work.
1:09:24–1:10:15	Truman in his office, where he is introduced to Vivian.
1:10:16–1:10:21	Truman mowing the lawn.
18 He's gone	
1:10:22–1:14:23	A night in the lunar room. Christof appears and asks for Truman. He seems to be in the basement sleeping, but Christof suspects something is wrong. So Marlon is sent to look for Truman and detects that Truman has escaped through a hole in the basement. Christof panics and cuts transmission.
1:14:24–1:14:38	The viewers in the Truman Bar and the old ladies are shocked that transmission is cut.
1:14:39–1:17:44	There is panic in the control room. In Seahaven everybody is searching for Truman. Since it is too dark Christof orders to cue the sun although it is far too early for that.
19 Setting sail	
1:17:45–1:18:39	Finally they find Truman on a sailing boat and resume transmission.
1:18:40–1:18:55	The viewers are betting on Truman's escape.
1:18:56–1:19:59	Christof decides to send a ferry after Truman, but nobody can start the engine, because they are just actors.
20 Cue the storm	
1:20:00–1:24:10	So Christof creates a storm, a series of waves and lightning to stop Truman from escaping – but in vain. Truman is so determined that he does not even give up when his boat capsizes. The viewers feel pity for him and join his struggle to escape.
21 The sky's the limit	
1:24:11–1:28:06	Truman has survived. He continues to sail and suddenly bumps into the artificial horizon. He gets off the boat, walks along the wall and comes to a staircase.
22 Who am I?	
1:28:07–1:30:57	As Truman gets to the exit, Christof wants to talk to him. He explains to him that he is the creator of a TV show giving hope, joy and inspiration to the world and that Truman is part of it. He tells him about important steps in his life he has observed and that Seahaven is his home he cannot leave.
23 Good afternoon, good evening and good night	
1:30:56–1:32:08	When he asks Truman to speak, because he is 'on air' Truman greets the audience again saying: Good afternoon, good evening and good night and leaves the show. Sylvia gets up and runs to Truman. Transmission is cut.
Credits	
1:32:09	

Viewing comprehension

With the help of guiding questions try to decipher the meaning of the sequences. Here are possible questions for each sequence.

1. Who and what is introduced in the first sequence?
2. What comes down from the sky and crashes a few inches from Truman's car?
3. How does the radio comment on this event?
4. What is Truman secretly enquiring about at the office?
5. What happens when Truman is sent to Harper Island?
6. What is Meryl advertising when she comes home?
7. What does Truman tell Marlon?
8. What is Truman trying to memorize and what happens on the beach?
9. What does Truman tell Meryl?
10. Who does Truman meet on his way to the office?
11. How does Truman's mother react to this incident?
12. What does Truman do with the old trunk?
13. What is Meryl advertising again?
14. What is Truman's mood like when looking at his old things?
15. How does Truman get acquainted with Lauren and Meryl?
16. Describe the sequence in the library.
17. What happens on the beach?
18. What picture is Truman trying to reconstruct?
19. What mysterious things happen on Truman's way to work?
20. What about the secret room?
21. What does Truman tell Marlon when they are together on the beach?

22 What does Truman discover when he again looks at the wedding photos?

23 What does Truman find out when he follows Meryl on her way to the hospital?

24 What happens in the travel agency?

25 What happens at the bus station?

26 Why does Truman want Meryl to get into his car and what happens when the two try to leave Seahaven?

27 Why does Truman panic when they arrive at the police blockade?

28 Why does Meryl show unexpected behaviour when she quarrels with Truman?

29 How does Christof prompt Marlon when he assures Truman of his friendship and introduces the father-son reunion?

30 What is Trutalk?

31 What is presented by Mr Michaelson?

32 What does Christof reveal in the interview with Michaelson?

33 Why does Christof touch the face of the sleeping Truman?

34 Who is introduced to Truman when he's back at his office?

35 What happens in the lunar room when they realize that the sleeping Truman is only a fake?

36 What does Christof order to cue although it's too early for that?

37 Where do they finally find Truman?

38 What does Christof decide to do when his first attempt to send out a ferry after Truman fails?

39 What is the viewers' reaction when they observe Truman's fight for life against the storm Christof has cued?

40 Why did Christof stop the storm?

41 What happens when Truman reaches the artificial horizon?

42 How does Truman react in the end when Christof tries to persuade him to stay in Seahaven?

How Truman smelled a rat

1 When a police officer calls Truman's name, he panics, runs away terrified and is finally caught.

2 Truman enters a building and discovers a secret room of the set behind a lift. He is thrown out of the building.

3 Truman is on his way to work and hears mysterious voices from the radio. The voice seems to be describing his route – suddenly people are acting strangely.

4 Back on the beach a shower directly rains on Truman. He jumps from side to side and is followed by the shower.

5 On his way to his office he meets his dad, but when Truman wants to talk to him, he is dragged into a bus and taken away. Truman tries to follow him – in vain.

6 He discovers that Meryl kept her fingers crossed on one of the wedding photos.

7 A large glass object falls from the sky and lands with a crash only a few inches from Truman's car.

8 There is a traffic jam. Truman pretends to calm down, drives back, changes his mind again and finds that there is no traffic jam any more.

9 Truman wants to book a flight to Fiji in the travel agency, but there are no flights for a month.

10 He continues to sail and suddenly bumps into the artificial horizon.

11 Truman is at the bus station, from where he wants to get to Chicago. However, the bus does not leave because of engine trouble.

12 Meryl calls a hidden cam for help, which makes Truman even more suspicious.

13 Meryl comes home from work and approaches Truman in his car. Truman predicts that in a minute they will see a lady on a bike followed by a man with flowers and a dented VW-Beetle.

14 Truman follows her to the hospital in his pyjamas, but the staff try to stop him.

■ Arrange the cue cards in the correct order and explain how Truman found out about his life on TV.

Truman

In case I don't see you …
good afternoon,
good evening
and good night!

Truman is the star of a TV show that is on for 24 hours a day, 365 days a year. There are about 5,000 cameras to observe everything he is doing.

■ Look at the stills and explain how this is made clear to the viewer by means of film language.

www.cartoonstock.com

0:03:49

0:08:07

0:52:10

0:52:20

0:57:42

0:59:14

0:59:21

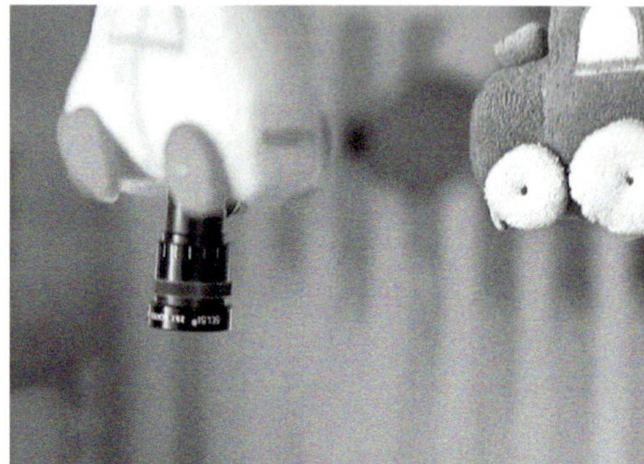

1:02:47

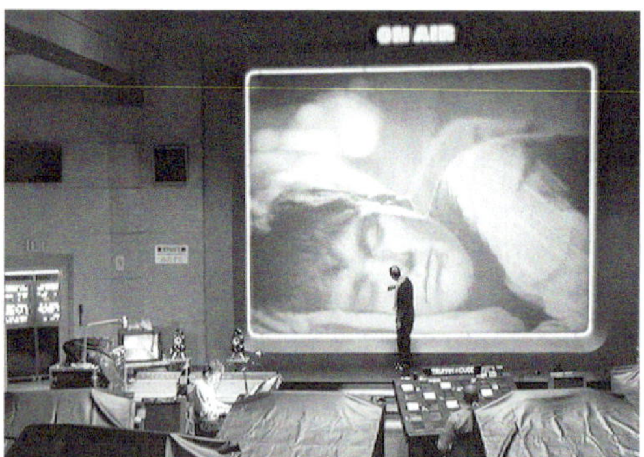

1:06:58

1:09:35

Truman ... in the mirror

In three sequences we find Truman not filmed directly, but through a mirror.

■ **1** Look at the stills: Why might the director have chosen to film the sequence through the mirror?

0:30:57

Truman acting strangely and walking around the town after he heard mysterious voices on the radio.
[0:29:28–0:33:10]

■ **2** Analyse this sequence and describe how Truman's growing confusion is shown with filmic devices. Pay special attention also to the sound.
► Don't forget to start your *viewing log* (www.cornelsen.de/abi-e) to keep track of the section as well as of striking filmic devices.

0:34:36

Truman in Marlon's shop after he discovered a secret room of the set and was thrown out of the building.
[0:33:11–0:34:40]

0:48:09

Truman has found out that something is wrong with the world he lives in. So he spontaneously wants to leave Seahaven with his wife.
[0:43:49–0:49:06]

■ **3** Analyse the sequence. Pay special attention to how Meryl deals with this awkward situation. Pay attention to film language and the dialogue.

Father and son reunion [0:53:09–0:58:37]

In their conversation Marlon reassures Truman of his friendship by mentioning emotional details from their common childhood. He also emphasizes that he would never lie to his best friend and that there's no conspiracy in Seahaven.

0:53:11

Both are sitting on an unfinished bridge.

■ **1** What filmic devices are used to introduce the film's major characters (Marlon and Truman) and the location? ▸ Fill in your *viewing log* as you watch the sequence.

■ **2** Watch the sequence on the bridge and in the lunar room again. What is the function of the cuts from one place to another?

0:54:39

0:55:03

■ **3** What kind of shots are used here to show both protagonists and why?
What state is Truman in and what does the film show of Marlon?

Close-ups with the camera positioned nearly at the subject's eye level [0:56:37 / 0:56:42] prepare the way for the forthcoming reunion of father and son. Marlon gives a hand to his friend but the final image shows Truman all alone. He is frightened and curious about what will happen.

The reunion is opened.

■ **4** What filmic devices are used?

■ **5** We can't see the person's face: What kind of shot does the camera therefore switch to?

The identification remains uncertain – the sequence actually becomes more obscure: [0:56:44]

■ 6 Instead of getting even closer: What is Christof's directive to the camera people? What kind of shots are used now and what for?

Both Truman and the unknown person are getting closer:
[0:56:57] [0:57:00]

0:56:57

■ 7 What filmic means (camera position, editing) are used to show the rising tension?

■ 8 Why and how does the film show the viewers' reactions?

0:57:14

Close-up cut: What will happen to him?

0:57:15

Cut / button camera: It's dad!!!

Truman never stopped believing that his father was still alive and the viewers share his emotions. Cuts are continued...

0:57:20

0:57:24

Then comes the climax: The two persons have reached each other – the camera angle switches to parallel eye positions. Truman and his father can be identified and both start hugging each other.

0:57:25

The moment of embracing is captured by another camera switch.
Christof is shown heavily directing this sequence.

■ 9 Why does he reject a close-up? Why does he order music to be faded in?

At this moment of extreme tension and emotional suspense we see a variety of camera techniques being used, beginning with cuts from the lunar room to the bridge and ending in an extreme close-up of Truman's face: [0:57:29] [0:57:35] [0:57:42] [0:57:45]

Extreme close-up: Dad!!!

The emotional climax is overwhelming for the viewers – cuts document the impact of this sequence:

0:58:06

Even the crew in the lunar room are enthusiastic about the success of this sequence.
[0:57:58] [0:58:15]

Christof leaves the lunar room and is congratulated by two main sponsors of the show.

0:58:25

The *father and son reunion* can be regarded as the emotional climax of the film (alongside the episode when Truman fights the sea). With reference to the technical instructions, camera positions, etc., it is a masterpiece of stage directions which are clearly expressed by the instructions Christof gives to his team.

In these segments the viewers are confronted with a masterly display of congruence between dialogue and cinematic realization.

Meryl – Truman's beloved wife – is a central figure in the story. She is a nurse and regularly shows various items she has recently purchased.
Her role is essentially to act as Truman's wife and to have a child by him. But the more the viewer gets into the story, the more doubts grow over whether she really loves him.

0:13:03

The happiest day of their lives?

0:36:17

Doesn't she look beautiful? Isn't she seductive?

Yes! And she gets an extra of 10,000 dollars every time she sleeps with Truman.

And what about a baby for Grandma?

■ 1 Reconsider the development of Truman with regard to Meryl. Point out the sequences where both characters appear and note down Meryl's reactions. ▸ Use your *viewing log*.

In the end Christof tells the viewers in an interview that Meryl is about to leave the show and that a new romantic episode will soon begin for Truman.

■ 2 Having been dismissed Meryl explains why she left the show. What motives did she have?

■ 3 Truman was chosen out of five unwanted pregnancies and was the first child to be legally adopted by a corporation. Imagine if Meryl and Truman had a baby. It would be the first baby from a well-paid mother (actress) and a father legally adopted by a corporation. Just professional or morally perverse? What do you think?

Ideas for further projects:

■ Do you think Meryl is plausible/persuasive in the way she tries to excuse herself? Do you believe her?

■ Could you imagine playing a role like this, marrying a man you don't like, pretending a love you don't feel?

■ What do you think of Christof's idea of introducing a new romance in Truman's life – will it work?

■ And what about true love?

Lauren – also a TV addict?

0:58:48

■ **1** Describe the impression you get of Lauren in the still and explain how this impression is achieved.
► Don't forget to note your results in your *viewing log*.

■ **2** Look at the two other stills and watch the following sequences again. Make a list and collect arguments for and against Lauren being a TV addict just like the other spectators.

1:03:46

1:04:34

[0:18:06–0:28:18] Truman in the basement: Flashback of this encounter with Lauren/Sylvia
[0:58:33–0:58:53] Before the TV interview with Christof.
[1:03:45–1:06:08] Lauren's telephone conversation with Christof.
[1:30:18–1:31:30] Lauren watches Truman leave the show.

Addict	Not an addict

■ **3** Analyse onc of the sequences and explain how Lauren's affection for Truman is made clear to the spectator with the help of dialogue and the filmic devices.

Lauren tells her story

Lauren/Sylvia is an important character for Truman because through her he grows suspicious that something might be wrong about Seahaven and his world.

■ 1 Tell Lauren's story from her point of view and also explain why she continuously watches the show. Explain how her motivation differs from that of the other spectators.

- ★ When I first met Truman I ....
- ★ At college he was playing in a band and had only eyes for ...
- ★ When partying with other students I was dragged away because ...
- ★ In the library I persuaded him to ...
- ★ But the producers were quick and ...
- ★ It nearly broke my heart when ...
- ★ I kept watching the show because ...
- ★ When getting the chance to talk to Christof on the phone I ...
- ★ If only I could have ...
- ★ Seeing that he .... I felt really ....
- ★ When he finally left the show I was ...

Out of Seahaven

■ 1 Make up Truman's story – how he found the way out of Seahaven – with the help of the following close-ups. Think about the sequence it occurred in and how it contributes to the development of Truman's self-correction.

Truman cuts out pieces of different magazines in order to rebuild the face of the person he fell in love with.

The story of true love between Truman and Lauren (Silvia) is accompanied by a series of remarkable close-ups and extreme close-ups of eyes – Lauren's eyes and Truman's.

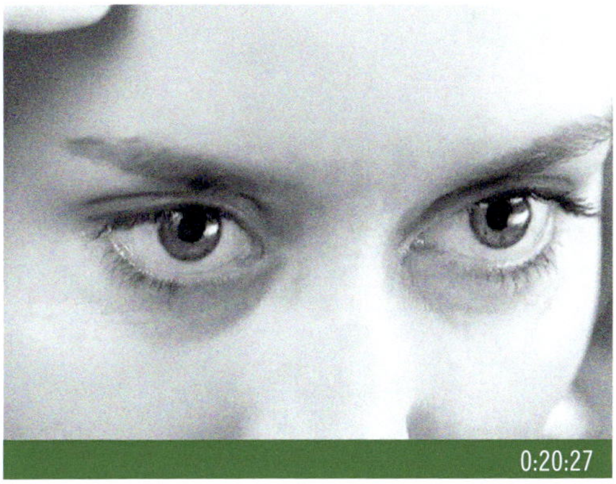

Extreme close-up: Extreme eyes

Get out of here. Come on and find me!

Is that really her?

The viewers of the show

1,7 million were there for his birth

A star is born

220 countries tuned in for his first step

The world stood still for that stolen kiss

A life broadcast live and unedited 24 hours a day, seven days a week to an audience around the globe

The headlines about *The Truman Show* underline its great popularity with a big audience around the whole world.

■ 1 Organize a conference with the makers of the show (Christof and two to three others) and discuss what kind of viewers you want to address with your programme.
Note down your ideas in a cluster.
Some aspects to think about:

Age group / Social status	Sex / Family status	Job / profession / Free-time activities

■ **2** Present your concept of the show and its potential viewers to the director of the television company that you want to sell it to.
The director, of course, may ask critical questions

■ **3** Look at the stills: [0:57:20] (p. 23), [0:58:00] (p. 24), [0:59:21] (p. 18). Explain why the people shown in the stills (do not) correspond with your idea of potential viewers of the show.

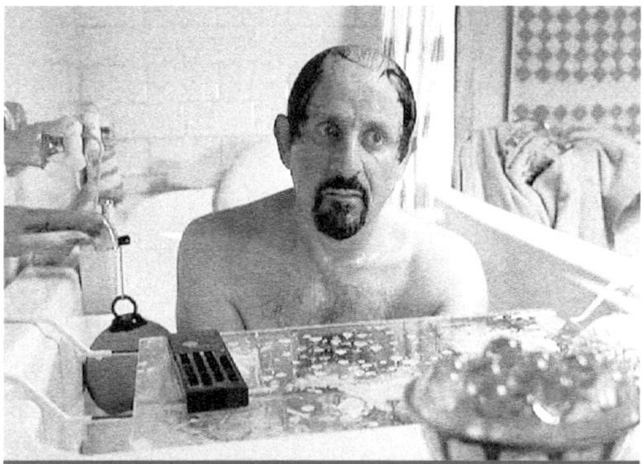

1:30:47

1:23:47

■ **4** Watch (some of) the sequences in the box again.
Analyse how the viewers of *The Truman Show* are characterized. In doing so describe the behaviour of the characters, analyse the filmic devices and the dialogue.
▸ Note your results in your *viewing log*.

[0:13:41–0:13:51]	The car park attendants	
[0:18:27–0:18:46]	The waitresses at the Truman Bar	
[0:26:46–0:27:05]	The waitresses at the Truman Bar (commenting on the same scene as before)	
[0:43:36–0:43:51]	At the Truman Bar: Waiters and customers	
[0:57:11–0:58:08]	Viewers' reactions to the reunion of father and son	
	[0:57:11–0:57:15]	Waitresses at the Truman Bar
	[0:57:17–0:57:20]	The old ladies
	[0:57:59–0:58:08]	Different groups
[0:58:51–0:59:41]	Global interest in *The Truman Show*	
[0:59:51–1:00:05]	Different groups watching the interview with Christof	
[1:06:09–1:06:20]	The man in the bath	
[1:14:22–1:14:38]	Reactions to the cut transmission: Truman Bar and old ladies	
[1:20:00–1:24:10]	Truman's escape	
	[1:21:25–1:21:27]	The man in the bath
	[1:22:07–1:22:10]	At the Truman Bar
	[1:22:12–1:22:15]	The man in the bath
	[1:23:46–1:23:49]	At the Truman Bar
[1:30:18–1:32:07]	Truman finally leaves the show	
	[1:30:43–1:30:51]	Different groups
	[1:31:31–1:31:48]	Different groups
	[1:32:00–1:32:07]	Car park attendants

Are you addicted to the media?

Note: Time spent on the computer for homework purposes does not count!

	Question	Yes	No
1.	Does your family have more than one TV set?		
2.	Are you in front of a screen for more than 2 hours per day?		
3.	Do you sometimes have trouble getting TV or video game jingles out of your head?		
4.	Is there a TV/video game/computer playing in your home much or all of the time?		
5.	Do you have a TV, video game, and/or computer in your bedroom?		
6.	Is it easy for you to turn off the TV/video game in the middle of a favourite show/game?		
7.	Do you ever rush home, ditching[1] friends and family, to catch a favourite TV show, play video games, or go on the computer?		
8.	Do you frequently eat meals while in front of the TV, video games, or computer?		
9.	Have you ever caught yourself unintentionally mimicking a TV or video game character?		
10.	Do you talk to and play with your friends more than you watch TV, play video games, and play with computers?		
11.	Can you turn the TV, computer, and video games OFF right now and leave them off for three days?		
12.	Do you ever mindlessly surf through TV channels or the Internet?		
13.	Do you need TV, video games, or a computer to relax after a rough day?		
14.	Do you feel edgy[2], anxious, or 'not right' if there is no TV, video game, or a computer playing?		
15.	Do you watch TV, play video games, and/or play on the computer more than spend time with your family?		
16.	Do you ever watch the TV, play video games, or surf the Internet longer than you intend to?		
17.	Do you feel you spend too much time with TV, video games, or computer?		
18.	Have you missed a special event with friends or family because you were watching a TV programme?		
19.	Have you ever tried to quit watching TV, playing video games, or going on computer, but were unsuccessful?		
20.	Do you have difficulty limiting the time you watch TV, play video games, or go on the computer?		

From www.TrashYourTV.com, Katherine Westphal 2007
Katherine Westphal created this quiz to raise awareness about the negative effects of TV and other media.

■ **5** Try to fill in the questionnaire for one of the viewers and explain why you decided to tick 'Yes' or 'No'. If the answer is not obvious, because the film does not say anything about it, discuss with a partner which answer is more likely.

■ **6** Would you call 'your' viewer a media addict? In your explanation you should not only refer to the evaluation underneath.

■ **7** Maybe you would like to find out if you are a media addict. Then do the test for yourself.

To calculate your score:

For all questions, except for 6, 10, and 11, give yourself 1 point for every 'Yes' and 0 points for every 'No'. For questions 6, 10, and 11 give yourself 0 points for every 'Yes' and 1 point for every 'No'. Add your total.

0–6: Great! Your TV, computer, and video games do not control your life. You do. But keep an eye on how much time you spend with these activities to make sure an addiction does not sneak up[3] on you.

7–14: It looks like you are moderately addicted to your TV, video games or computer. The good news is that, with a little effort, a list of fun non-screen activities, and a reasonable schedule you should be able to keep your addiction under control. Follow your dreams instead of staring at a screen.

15–20: You probably have a serious addiction problem. You may need to take extreme steps, including getting rid of your TV or video games, to get in control of your time. Start with the device that squanders[4] the most of your time. It may seem difficult, but life is too short to 'watch' it go by.

■ **8** After watching the sequences choose one of the viewers. Develop a character profile for this person. The following phrases might help you.

- ★ My name is ....
- ★ I work as .... / I do not work because ....
- ★ I am .... years old and live in / together with ...
- ★ I am married / single / divorced / a widow(er)
- ★ I watch the Truman show when ... / because ...
- ★ I (do not) think that I am a media addict because ...
- ★ What I like about the Truman Show is ...
- ★ To people like Lauren who criticize the show I say that
- ★ Now that the Truman show is no longer on TV, I ...

Top 10 reasons to become TV-FREE

1. People who watch 3 hours of TV per day are twice as likely to be obese[5] as people who watch less than 1 hour per day.
2. Average US parent spends only 38 minutes per week in meaningful conversation with children vs. 31½ hours per week watching TV.
3. TV viewing in children from 1 to 3 is associated with[6] ADHD[7] symptoms at age 7.
4. Viewing TV violence is the single strongest predictor[8] of aggression later in life, according to long-term study.
5. Children have witnessed up to 16,000 TV murders by the age of 18.
6. Viewers watch an average of 40,000 commercials per year.
7. Commercials aimed at children and young people influence an estimated $300 billion a year in sales via the 'Nag Factor'[9].
8. Students who watched an hour of TV per day or less scored the best on achievement tests.
9. TV is addictive.
10. The average American watches 4 hours 35 minutes of TV per day. There is simply so much else to do in life.

From www.TrashYourTV.com, Katherine Westphal 2007

1 *ditch (infml)* leave behind
2 *edgy* nervous and worried
3 *sneak up* come near someone/something quietly and slowly
4 *squander* waste
5 *obese* very fat in a way that is unhealthy
6 *be associated with* be related to
7 *ADHD* Attention deficit hyperactivity disorder
8 *predictor* something that shows what will happen in the future
9 *Nag Factor* degree to which parents' decisions to buy products are based on being nagged by their children

Christof – Creator of the show

■ 1 Write a short character sketch of Christof on the basis of the extracts from the film script and describe the impression that you get of him.

Christof: We've become tired of watching actors give us phoney emotions, bored with pyrotechnics and special effects. While the world he inhabits is counterfeit, there's nothing fake about Truman himself. No scripts, no cue cards. It is not always Shakespeare, but it's genuine.

Interviewer from Trutalk: We are honoured to bring you a rare and exclusive interview with the show's conceiver and creator. So come with us now. We go live to the Lunar Room on the 221st floor of the Omnicam Ecosphere. That's where we find the world's greatest televisionary, the designer and architect of a world within a world – Seahaven Island.

Interviewer: Before we begin I'd like to thank you on behalf of our audience for granting us this exclusive interview. We know how demanding your schedule is and we all know how jealously you guard your privacy.

Christof: He was curious from birth – premature by two weeks, as if he couldn't wait to get started.
Interviewer: Of course, his eagerness to leave his mother's womb also meant he was the one selected.

Christof: In competition with five other unwanted pregnancies – the casting of a show determined by an air date – he was the one who arrived on cue.
Interviewer: Why do you feel that Truman's never come close to discovering the true nature of his world?
Christof: We accept the reality of the world with which we're presented.

Christof: As the show expanded, naturally we were forced to manufacture ways to keep Truman in Seahaven – demonstrating that every venture is accompanied by a risk.

Sylvia: You are a liar and a manipulator and what you've done to Truman is sick.
Christof: Do you think that [...] you know what's right for him? Do you really think you are in a position to judge him? [...] I have given Truman the chance to lead a normal life. The world, the place you live in, is the sick place. Seahaven is the way the world should be. [...] He can leave at any time. If this was more than a vague ambition, if he was absolutely determined to discover the truth, there's no way we could prevent him. [...] I think what really distresses you, caller, is that, ultimately, Truman prefers his cell, as you call it.

Christof: I am determined that TV's first on-air conception will still take place.

1:00:08

Moses: For God's sake Christof. The whole world is watching. You can't let him die in front of a live audience.
Christof: He was born in front of a live audience.

Christof: Truman … you can speak. I can hear you.
Truman: Who are you?
Christof: I am the creator of a TV show that gives hope and joy and inspiration to millions.
Truman: Then who am I?
Christof: You're the star.
Truman: Was nothing real?
Christof: You were real. That's what made you so good to watch. Listen to me, Truman. There is no more truth out there than there is in the world I created for you. The same lies, the same deceit. But in my world you have nothing to fear. I know you better than you know yourself.
Truman: You never had a camera in my head.
Christof: You're afraid. That's why you can't leave. It's OK, Truman, I understand. I was watching you when you were born. I was watching you when you took your first step. I watched you on your first day of school. The episode when you lost your first tooth. You can't leave, Truman. You belong here. With me. Talk to me. Say something. Say something, damn it! You're on TV. You're live to the whole world.

■ **2** Watch [0:59:55–1:07:07] and [1:28:07–1:30:57]. To what extent would you say your impression of Christof has been generated with the help of the filmic devices?

1:00:29

1:02:13

1:28:41

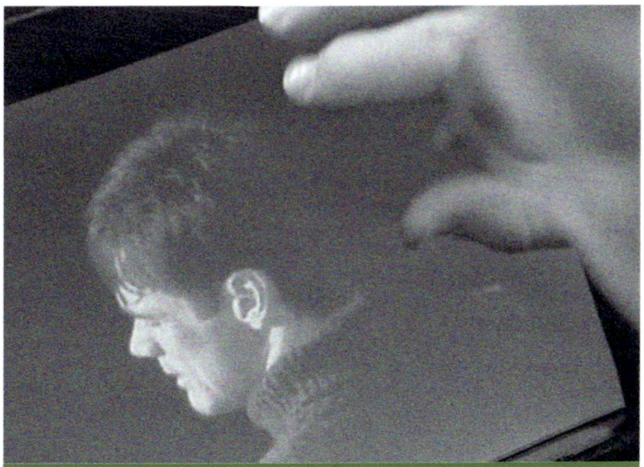
1:29:45

■ **3** Looking at the cartoon again: Discuss who you consider responsible for Truman's fate.

Product placement – How they finance the show

US networks cash in as advertisers turn to product placement

The *American Idol* judges sit with Coca-Cola cups on the table in front of them. The contestants in the new series of *The Apprentice* hang out in a Poggenpohl kitchen. The good guys in CSI: *Crime Scene Investigation* zap around[1] in GMC Yukon vehicles.

These are the latest and most visible signs of advertisers' fight against the growing power of the television viewer: the ability to edit out the commercials. TiVo, Sky+ and other digital recorders allow viewers to watch programmes without having to endure the advertisement breaks that are rife in US television.

As sales of these devices have grown – they are expected to be in 55m US homes by 2010 – so companies have looked to other ways to get their products onto the small screen. Their favourite method is what was once known by the quaint term[2] "product placement", but now goes under the somewhat more sinister[3] title of integrated or branded entertainment.

It was reported this week that spending by US advertisers on product placement had grown from $550m (about £310m) in 2004 to an expected $825m this year. The number of placements on television grew by 100% in the first quarter of the year, and a further 100% in the second quarter. "Product placement is like crack cocaine to the networks," said *Variety* magazine.

The leader is *The Contender*, which, according to Nielsen Media Research, had 7,500 instances of product placement in the first six months of the year.

The practice is also starting to take hold in the UK. Earlier this month the BBC was accused of breaching its guidelines[4] after it was reported that an agency had paid £40,000 to advertise products within BBC programmes. Last week the EU said it would approve product placement in programmes, provided certain guidelines were followed.

Product placement typically takes one of three forms: it can be the free gift of an item used, for example, for set decoration; it can take the form of a barter arrangement[5] in which a product will be given to a programme in return for a shot or placement of the company's logo; or it can be a more straightforward financial transaction, in which a company pays to have its product included in a scene or threaded[6] through an entire programme.

One of the most blatant[7] examples came on the Oprah Winfrey show last year, when 276 audience members found the keys to a new car under their seat. Subsequent research showed that 95% of Americans knew about the promotion.

But while advertisers are spending millions getting their products on television shows, there is no way of telling if the branding filters through to sales. For that reason there is no set rate for how much production companies should charge advertisers.

At the top end of the scale is Mark Burnett, the executive producer of *The Apprentice* and *Survivor*, who charges up to $5m to weave a product into an hour-long edition of *The Apprentice*. His latest creation, *The Apprentice: Martha Stewart*, has more than 20 integration partners, including Proctor & Gamble, General Electric, General Motors and brands such as Nestlé, Dell and L'Oreal.

But there is a potential downside. The Delta Faucet Company was thrilled that one of its shower fittings was to be featured on *CSI: Miami*. It was not so thrilled when it saw the episode: a character slips and dies after hitting her head on a Delta showerhead.

The Guardian, Friday 30 September 2005

1 *zap around* here: drive in
2 *quaint* unusual and attractive
3 *sinister* making you feel that something evil, dangerous, or illegal will happen
4 *breaching its guidelines* breaking its rules
5 *barter arrangement* a system of exchanging goods or services
6 *threaded...* here: carefully placed in different scenes of the programme
7 *blatant* something bad that is *blatant* is very clear and easy to see, but the person responsible for it does not seem embarrassed or ashamed

l. 13 rife = widely spread

■ **1** Point out why 'product placement' or 'branded entertainment' is becoming more and more popular.

■ **2** Explain the sentence 'Product Placement is like crack cocaine to the networks'.

■ **3** State briefly the three different forms of product placement.

■ **4** Outline the Europeans' attitude towards product placement.

■ **5** Summarize the problems that are connected with product placement.

■ **6** Analyse the author's attitude towards product placement and explain how it gets clear in the text.

Product placement in 'The Truman Show'

1:03:19

■ **7** Look at the stills: [1:03:07], [1:03:16], [0:51:50], [0:52:41] and read the extract from the interview with Christof (p. 42). Then explain how product placement works in the film.

■ **8** Find other examples for product placement in the film.

Interviewer: The show has generated enormous revenues, now equivalent to the Gross National Product of a small country.
Christof: People forget it takes the population of an entire country to keep the show running.
Interviewer: Since the show is on 24 hours a day without commercial interruption all those staggering revenues are generated by product placement.
Christof: That's true. Everything on the show is for sale.

Statement by Ken Sanes about product placement in 'The Truman Show':

The Truman Show's depiction of the way product placement is woven into Truman's life is an effective satire* on the commercialization of our own lives. Today, forms of entertainment are commercials; commercials are forms of entertainment; and the boundary between both, and the rest of life, is becoming blurred.
Taking the point one or two steps further, we can say that the media would have us live inside a world of fiction that is the most glorious commercial ever devised, for a system in which life, sales, and entertainment are interfused. 'Product placement' and testimonials for this emerging system of entertainment-marketing capitalism are being seamlessly woven into our lives.

http://www.transparencynow.com/truprod.htm

■ **9** Explain the statement.

■ **10** Discuss if and to what extent the film satirizes the commercialisation of our own lives by carefully analysing selected sequences from the film.
Among others you could refer to the following sequences:
[0:08:49–0:09:29] [0:51:16–0:52:44] [1:02:55–1:03:22]
▸ *Viewing log*

■ **11** Comment on the suggestion made in the statement by Ken Sanes and in the film that our lives are commercialized. In doing so also try to give examples from German TV programmes.

---

* *Satire* Literature which exhibits or examines vice and folly and makes them appear ridiculous or contemptible. Though the distinction is not always clear, satire differs from the comic in having a purpose: it is directed against a person or a type, and it is usually morally censorious.

Utopia

UTOPIA

Among the classic Utopian models, Plato's *Republic* is by far the most important. It became a literary guidepost. The first great successor was Sir Thomas More, the Renaissance humanist, who gave a name to a whole literature with his work *Utopia* (1516).

The word *Utopia* is a pun since its literal meaning is either nowhere (from the Greek outopia) or good place (from the Greek eutopia). From that origin we can determine two modes of *Utopia*: Utopias of escape and Utopias of reconstruction.

Since the Renaissance the term *Utopia* has been used for an ideal society with a fictitious character. The Utopian society shows a clear distance to the real, historical world. The relationship between Utopia and the real world can be defined as an alternative draft to reality. Utopia is therefore an ideal place as well as a criticism of the existing real world.

Another criterion of Utopia is its *Inselcharakter*. All Utopian states are located on an island, or at least they possess characteristics of isolation, remoteness or insularity. They can't interact with the real world since they are separated by rules, laws and/or natural conditions or obstacles.

A Utopian state can therefore be called self-contained, based on clear, logical and vivid regulations, a construction that does not exist in reality but shows a model for alternative life.

Recent works have constructed an anti-Utopia, or dystopia, which is mainly a portrayal of society controlled by a certain authority.

In the tradition of dystopian novels we find George Orwell's *1984*, Aldous Huxley's *Brave New World* and Ray Bradbury's *Fahrenheit 451*.

For further information see: Paul Maloney, Utopia and Dystopia, Cornelsen 2008.

■ 1 With the help of the following voices try to evaluate the Utopian character of *The Truman Show*. Give examples where the insularity of the Utopian world is interrupted.
▸ Make notes in your *viewing log*.

... there's nothing fake about Truman himself. ... it's genuine. [0:00:37]

... no difference between private life and public life. My life is the Truman Show. It's a truly blessed life. [0:01:21]

... It's all real. It's merely controlled. [0:01:57]

What's coming down from heaven? A spotlight?!

The whole world is ... a stage?

... where is the way out?

The bridge to another world?

... transmitted all over the world!

A fictitious world!

The omni-cam – Christof is always watching you!

It's a model world!

The link to the real world?

The first contact ...

Realizing everything has been a fake!

Interview with Christof

Michaelson: Equivalent to the GNP of a small country.
Christof: It takes the population of an entire country to keep it running. [...]
Christof: Seahaven is the way the world should be.

■ 1 Take this core part of the interview from the film and try to develop an alternative ending in which the reporter doubts Christof's words – although there has been quite a remarkable economic success – insisting that *The Truman Show* still remains a dystopia.

■ 2 With regard to the pros and cons depicted in *The Truman Show*: Discuss whether the concept of Seahaven is an example for a utopian or dystopian society.

Truman: The camera never sleeps

Film review

The Truman Show is *Candid Camera*[1] run amok, a sugar-spun nightmare of pop paranoia that addresses the end of privacy, the rise of voyeurism and the violation of the individual. Not that there's anything wrong with that.

This show-within-the-show makes for a parody all by itself, but it is couched in an even more subversively entertaining satire. One of the smartest, most inventive movies in memory, it manages to be as endearing[2] as it is provocative.

The plot revolves around the world's most popular television show, a hybrid of reality-based programming that follows the every move of Truman Burbank (Jim Carrey), who made his unwitting debut via sonogram[3] 30 years ago and has been under 24-hour scrutiny[4] ever since.

His wholesome hometown of Seahaven is really a vast soundstage equipped with 5,000 hidden cameras. His friends, neighbors, even his toxically cheerful wife (Laura Linney) are all actors, genuine as Naugahyde[5]. But Truman has yet to figure it out because it's the only world he's ever seen. He's grown up on television.

In a way, the same thing could be said for the rest of us, which is exactly the point of this cautionary fable superbly directed by Peter Weir and written by Andrew Niccol, director of last year's *Gattaca*. Though every bit as dark as that kindred portrait of genetic fascism, this yarn[6] possesses a playful spirit.

As a send-up of media culture, it's more akin to *Forrest Gump* than 1976's ranting *Network*[7].

In this creepy not-too-distant future, *The Truman Show* has attracted 1.7 billion viewers, who enjoy watching the clueless patsy[8]. The program's amiably goofy[9] protagonist, however, has stagnated in the sunny surrealism of his sitcom Eden. Housed in a snow dome world created by the 'televisionary' Christof (Ed Harris), synthetic Seahaven offers neither surprises nor challenges for its naive captive.

But Truman accepts his world's modest pleasures, minor frustrations and predictable rhythms without question. Then one morning as he sets out for work, something odd happens. A klieg light drops from the sky and crashes in front of his gingerbread house.

Truman approaches it cautiously, like the apes before the monolith in *2001: A Space Odyssey*, squints up[10] at the blue sky in wonderment and for the first time begins to take stock[11] of his life: dull job, insufferable Stepford wife[12] and frustration at every turn in his plan to flee to Fiji.

1 *Candid Camera* Name of a TV show similar to Verstehen Sie Spaß? on German TV
2 *endearing* likeable, loveable
3 *sonogram* an image of an unborn baby in the mother's womb
4 *scrutiny* observance
5 *Naugahyde* a well-known brand of artificial leather
6 *yarn (infml.)* here: story of adventures
7 *Network* a 1976 satirical film about a fictional television network, Union Broadcasting System (UBS), and its struggle with poor ratings.
8 *patsy (infml.)* someone who is easily tricked or decieved
9 *goofy (infml)* silly or stupid
10 *squint u* look at something with your eyes partly closed
11 *take stock of sth.* think carefully about the things that have happened in order to decide what to do next
12 *Stepford wife* The term 'Stepford Wife' is used to describe a woman who lives a blindly conforming life, remaining subservient to her husband and other authority figures while attempting to offend no-one.

Truman may not be mad as hell, but he's not going to take it anymore, either. Whether a victim of corporate avarice[13] or his own gullibility[14], one thing's for darned[15] sure: This boob[16] is determined to escape the tube.

If the film is a showcase for Carrey, who gives a performance of enormous charm and restraint, it's also a triumph for Harris as the misguided man behind the curtain. Linney plays the plastic wife with scary success. And even the smallest roles, like smarmy Harry Shearer's TV reporter, are deftly cast.

Who would have expected this from *The Cable Guy*? This splendid movie is about as far from *Dumb and Dumber* as *60 Minutes* is from *Jerry Springer*.

13 *avarice* greed
14 *gullibility* Gullible people are too ready to believe what other people tell them and can be tricked easily.
15 *darned (infml.)* damn
16 *boob (old-fashioned)* stupid or silly person

By Rita Kempley, from The Washington Post Company 1998: http://www.washingtonpost.com/wpsrv/style/longterm/movies/videos/trumanshowkempley.htm

■ **1** Summarize the author's opinion of the film.

■ **2** Analyse the language the author uses to make her point clear. Do you find this language suitable for a review?

■ **3** The author characterizes Truman more than once as a 'silly or stupid person'. Comment on her opinion. In doing so also give examples from the film to support your arguments.

■ **4** Analyse the structure of the review: In which passages do you learn something about the plot, the actors, the director, etc. and in which passages does the author express her opinion about the film?

■ **5** Collect useful phrases for writing a review from the given review.

■ **6** Write your own review of *The Truman Show*.

Director tries a fantasy as he questions reality

Interview with Peter Weir

Peter Weir was despondent[1]. It was 1995, and after directing acclaimed films like *The Year of Living Dangerously, Witness,* and *Dead Poets Society,* he was seeking his next project but finding every script either predictable or derivative[2].

'I remember finally saying, "Send me your broken scripts," ' said Mr. Weir, an Australian. 'Someone asked me what I was looking for, and I said, "I'm looking for trouble." '

He found what he wanted. His new film, '*The Truman Show,*' written by Andrew Niccol and starring Jim Carrey, is the most subversive[3] studio film of the summer. It is bound to stir controversy and serve as a touchstone for cultural debate, as *Network*[4] did more than 20 years ago.

In the fantasy, which opens on June 5, Mr. Carrey plays Truman Burbank, who lives in a picture-postcard town called Seahaven that is a little too perfect. In truth, Seahaven is the huge set of the highest-rated television show in the nation, and Truman Burbank has, from birth, been its star. Only he doesn't know it. The television show is Truman's life, and his reality. His family, neighbors and friends are all actors. Slowly, Truman realizes that he is imprisoned and must flee.

Mr. Weir said that the script, which was sent to him by the film's producer, Scott Rudin, haunted him for several weeks.

'The freshness of the concept and the dialogue appealed to me immensely,' Mr. Weir, 53, a modest man with a soft smile, said at lunch at a hotel in Beverly Hills. 'But I kept thinking: "How do I do this? How do I go about it?" I tried to get rid of the idea of doing it, but it reached a point where it was driving me nuts."

'It was like trying to pick up a hedgehog. It was bristling with metaphors, and I was concerned about whether or not I could take the audience with me on this journey that would break some of the conventions of mainstream movie making. It's not your regular movie. To some degree, the film subverts the movie form itself.'

What finally led him to make the film for Paramount was a meeting with Mr. Carrey, who had already read the script and was seeking a serious role after hit comedies like *Dumb and Dumber* and *Ace Ventura, Pet Detective.* (The fact that Mr. Weir had turned Robin Williams into a dramatic actor in *Dead Poets Society* appealed to Mr. Carrey.)

Mr. Weir flew to Los Angeles from his home in Sydney to meet Mr. Carrey. 'We hit it off right from the start,' the director said. 'I was honest with him, saying I really didn't know how I'd go about it. But I played him a piece of music from Pink Floyd's *Wish You Were Here* album, which I thought summed up the film effectively with the lyrics: 'So you think you can tell heaven from hell? Blue skies from pain? Can you tell a green field from a cold steel rail? So you think you can tell.' "

1 *despondent* extremely unhappy and without hope
2 *derivative* not new or invented, but copied or taken from something else
3 *subversive* subversive ideas, activities, etc. are secret and intended to damage an established system
4 *Network* a 1976 satirical film about a fictional television network, Union Broadcasting System (UBS), and its struggle with poor ratings.

[...]

What gives the film an eerie prescience[5], he said, is how television increasingly blurs the line between fact and fiction, reality and drama. From the days of television icons like *Ozzie and Harriet* and *I Love Lucy* through contemporary shows like *Seinfeld, Ellen* or *The Larry Sanders Show*[6], fantasy and real life overlap.

Even more significant, Mr. Weir said, is the hazy nature of news. On the very day that Paramount began promoting *The Truman Show* in the Los Angeles *Times*, television viewers, many of them children, were riveted[7] by coverage of a freeway chase in which a man set himself and his dog on fire and then shot himself.

'One of the writers in the newspaper said that the only way that he knew this was real, as opposed to unreal, was that there was a dog dying in the front seat of the vehicle, too,' Mr. Weir said.'And you don't see dogs killed on television in fictional shows.'

[...]

By Bernard Weinraub, 1998: http://www.nytimes.com/1998/05/21/movies/director-tries-a-fantasy-as-he-questions-reality.html

5 *eerie* strange and frightening, *prescience* prediction of the future
6 *Ozzie and HarrietI love Lucy, Seinfeld, Ellen, The Larry Sanders Show* American sitcoms
7 *be riveted* be so interested in something that you keep looking at it

■ **1** Give reasons why Peter Weir decided to make the film *The Truman Show* after desperately seeking his next project for quite a while.

■ **2** Explain why Jim Carrey was interested in playing the role of Truman Burbank.

■ **3** Explain how Weir describes the nature of TV and list the examples he gives.

■ **4** Explain the meaning of the title of the article: *Director tries a fantasy as he questions reality.*

So you think you can tell heaven from hell?
Blue skies from pain?
Can you tell a green field from a cold steel rail?
So you think you can tell.

■ **5** Discuss whether the lyrics of Pink Floyd's song *Wish You Were Here* really sum up the film effectively as Weir claims:
Give reasons for your answer.

Fishbowl discussion

A *fishbowl* conversation is a form of dialogue that can be used when discussing topics within large groups.

For this discussion 8 chairs plus 1 for the moderator are arranged in an inner circle. This is the fishbowl. The remaining chairs are arranged in a circle outside the fishbowl. The 8 chairs in the inner circle are reserved for: Truman, Christof, Meryl, Marlon, Truman's mother, Truman's father, Lauren and the moderator. One chair remains empty.

After preparing their role-groups (one group for each character), one participant of each group either volunteers or is selected to fill the fishbowl, while the rest of the group sit on the chairs outside the fishbowl.

Then the moderator introduces the topic and the participants start discussing it. The audience outside the fishbowl listen in on the discussion. If they want to ask a question or want to contribute something to the discussion they are allowed to occupy the empty chair and say what they want to say. After that they must leave the fishbowl again.

Variation: If the group members get the impression that their 'fish' has forgotten something or cannot make his/her point clear, they can stand behind their 'fish'. The fish then has to leave the bowl and the new volunteer takes over.

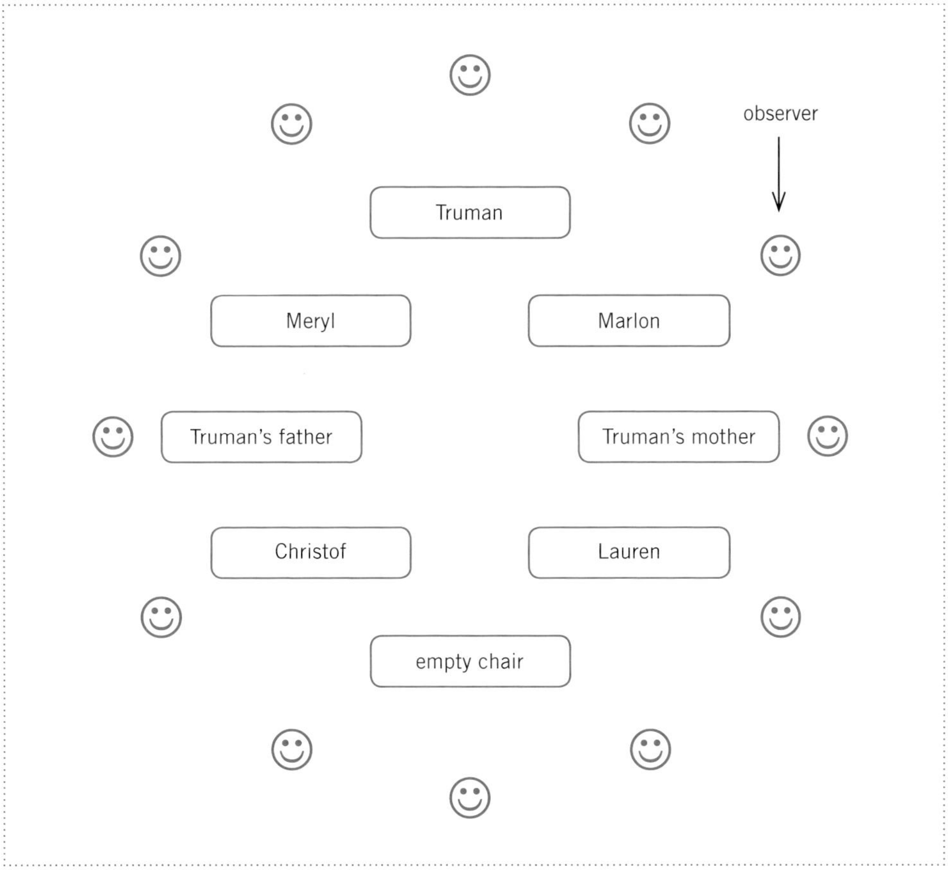

Preparation

The characters

■ 1 Get into 7 groups. Each group is responsible for one character:
Truman, Christof, Truman's mother, Truman's father, Meryl, Lauren, Marlon.

■ 2 Write a character profile for your person: Who are you? What happened to you? Why did you act the way you acted? How did you feel in certain situations?, etc.

■ 3 Imagine what your character has to say to the others: Is he/she thankful? Why? Does he/she want to reproach or blame someone or justify himself/herself for what he/she has done? Why? What does he/she want to ask the others?

The moderator

Your tasks during the discussion are the following:

■ 4 Welcome the participants of the discussion and explain what the discussion will be about.

■ 5 Explain the rules:
- The participants are not allowed to communicate with the 'observers' and vice versa.
- The participants should first introduce themselves in the first round: Who are they? What happened to them?
- The participants are not allowed to interrupt each other or to be rude.

■ 6 What you have to do during the discussion:
- Get the discussion going by calling on one of the participants to start the first round (see above).
- Open the second round by calling on one of the participants to start with the argumentation.
- Ensure that each person in the circle is allowed to speak, and that no one dominates the discussion.
- You will call to order if necessary.Interrupt the participants if they do not speak to the topic.
- Try to motivate the conversation when it gets stuck or loses substance by giving an impulse with a provocative question or by calling one of the observers to sit on the empty chair or to change places with one 'fish'.

■ 7 When time is up, finish the discussion by giving a final statement and summarizing the results. Thank the participants for the discussion.

Evaluation

First the participants say how they felt being in the circle.
With the help of the observation sheet, the observers can give feedback to the participants of the discussion. It should be clear before the discussion who observes whom.

Fishbowl discussion – Evaluation sheet for observers

	🙂	😐	🙁
Language			
Use of English: Pronunciation / grammar / vocabulary / fluency			
Manner of speaking: Loudness / speed / clarity			
Argumentation			
Are the arguments put forward in accordance with how the character is presented in the film?			
Does the speaker mention all the important points?			
Does the speaker (not) deviate from the topic?			
Does the speaker respond to arguments that are brought forward by others?			
Does the speaker listen to the others and allow others to make their point?			

Film evaluation

■ Answer the following questions using specific details from the film.

- How is the setting established in the film?
- How are the main characters introduced in the film?
- How is the conflict introduced?
- Describe a scene that worked well.
- Describe a scene that could be improved. Describe how.
- What is the climax? How do the filmmakers lead up to it?
- What's the message of the film?
- Would you recommend this film to future cinema classes? Why/why not? Be fair.
- Would you recommend this film to friends? Why/why not? Be fair.

Emotional response to the film:

Purpose/aim of the film as you see it:

Final verdict:

☐ very favourable ☐ favourable

☐ unfavourable ☐ uncertain

Film analysis in group work

■ How does the film work to subvert viewers' conventional cinematic expectations? Circle the terms in parentheses you are discussing:

Photography (shot, focus, frame, angle, movement, space, sets, lighting, colour)

Sound (music, dialogue, silence, language, synchronicity, sound effects)

Editing (order, transition, cuts, duration, rhythm, continuity, disjuncture, montage, motifs)

Narration (story/plot, dramatic appeal, motivation, logic, closure, point of view)

Other (self-reference, realism/representation, art, politics, values/ideology, historical context)

Acknowledgements

Texts
p. 34 *Media Addiction Quiz for Teens: Are you addicted to your TV, video games, or computer?*
p. 36 *Top 10 reasons to become TV-FREE,* from: www.TrashYourTV.com, © Katherine Westphal, 2007
p. 37 ff. *The Truman Show:* extract from the film script written by Andrew M. Niccol, © 1998, Andrew M. Niccol, http://www.imsdb.com/scripts/Truman-Show,-The.html
p. 40 *US Networks Cash in as Advertisers Turn to Product Placement,* from: *The Guardian,* September 30, 2005, © Guardian News & Media Ltd 2005
p. 47 f. *'Truman': The Camera Never Sleeps* by Rita Kempley, from: *The Washington Post online,* June 5, 1998, © 1998 The Washington Post. All rights reserved. Used by permission and protected by the Copyright Laws of the United States. The printing, copying, redistribution, or retransmission of the Material without express written permission is prohibited. http://www.washingtonpost.com/wpsrv/style/longterm/movies/videos/trumanshowkempley.htm.
p. 49 f. *Director Tries a Fantasy As He Questions Reality* by Bernard Weinraub, from *The New York Times,* May 21, 1998 © 1998 The New York Times. All rights reserved. Used by permission and protected by the Copyright Laws of the United States. The printing, copying, redistribution, or retransmission of the Material without express written permission is prohibited. http://www.nytimes.com/1998/05/21/movies/director-tries-a-fantasy-as-he-questions-reality.html

Illustrations
Cover: Stairway to the sky © Andrzej/Fotolia; ship © LFL/shotshop.com.
pp. 6, 16–28, 30, 31, 33, 38, 39, 41, 43–45 All stills taken from *The Truman Show,* a film by Peter Weir (with Jam Carrey, Laura Linney et alii) © 1998 Paramount Pictures. Courtesy of Universal Studios Licensing LLLP.
pp. 4, 34, 37 Cartoons by Nicholson from The Australian www.nicholsoncartoons.com.au
p. 16 www.CartoonStock.com © Kjell Nilsson-Maki